Today in the Forest

Today in the Forest

Poems by Cindy Rinne

Images by Toti O'Brien

MOONRISE PRESS

Copyright Information

Today in the Forest **by Cindy Rinne and Toti O'Brien**

This book is published by Moonrise Press

P.O. Box 4288, Los Angeles - Sunland, CA 91041-4288, www.moonrisepress.com; info@moonrisepress.com

Manufactured in the United States of America

The Library of Congress Publication Data
Rinne, Cindy (b. 1954) and O'Brien, Toti (b. 1959)
[Title] Today in the Forest (in English)
46 pages (vi pp. + 40 pp.) 15.2 cm x 22.9 cm.
Written in English.

ISBN 978-1-945938-43-6 (paperback)
ISBN 978-1-945938-44-3 (eBook in ePub format)
ISBN 978-1-945938-45-0 (eBook in PDF format)

10 9 8 7 6 5 4 3 2 1

Table of Contents

Poems by Cindy Rinne
Images by Toti O'Brien

Part I - Moon Goddess

Part II - Crystalwind's Family

Part I

Moon Goddess

Anahita Speaks Today in the Forest

I wear a golden crown and adore rushing streams as keeper of the waters. One aspen leaf speaks kind words to my horses. Its branch intersects another on a sky chart over Venus. Time to ride my chariot to observe plants adjusting to the hot, thick atmosphere on a planet whose long rotation swirls in the opposite direction. I glide the jet streams. My wetness resists burning to visit a cosmic garden.

Greetings, my children.

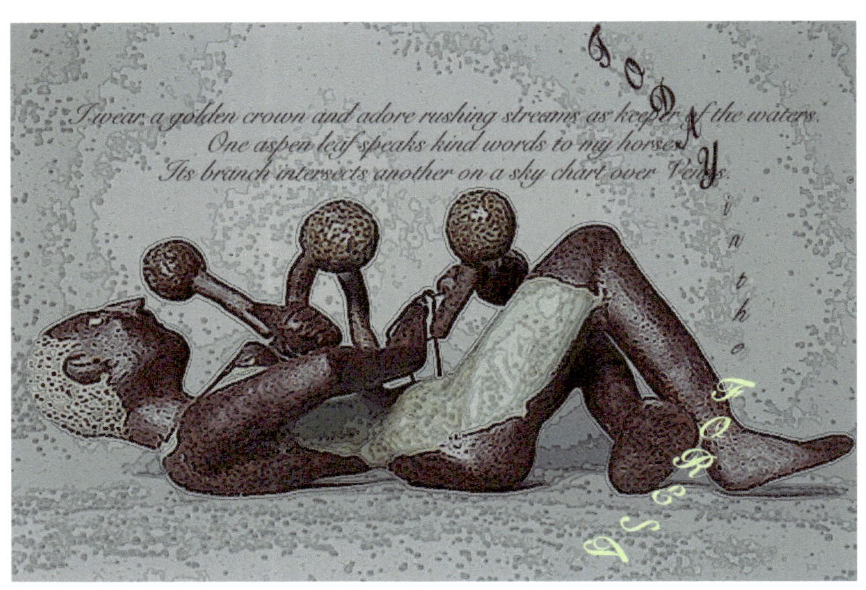
I wear a golden crown and adore rushing streams as keeper of the waters.
One aspen leaf speaks kind words to my horses.
Its branch intersects another on a sky chart over Venus.
TODAY in the FOREST

Presence/Absence

Wolf-people originated near lakes. Body of a wolf with a human face. Candlelight and stars greeted them each night. Reflections of golden aspens revealed day.

Moon goddess, Anahita appeared and said, *Elk are eating the aspen bark. Unknown disease enters exposed places.*

My trees are dying. The Candlepeople will be next. They must have a canopy of leaves.

How can we help? the wolf-people asked.

Select one Candleman to survive. I will instill a lightning bolt within black bear to generate a Candlewoman in the future.

She continued, *One day you will walk on two legs with wolf spirit inside. Remember your language.*

Anahita's Horses

Some days wine-color stallion calms down
And speaks of running wild.

Some days roan filly is a quiet mist–
Plants, birds, and trees rest.

Some days sunset coral mustang converses
with the sun about the day.

Some days silver ice protects the animals
before winter's thaw.

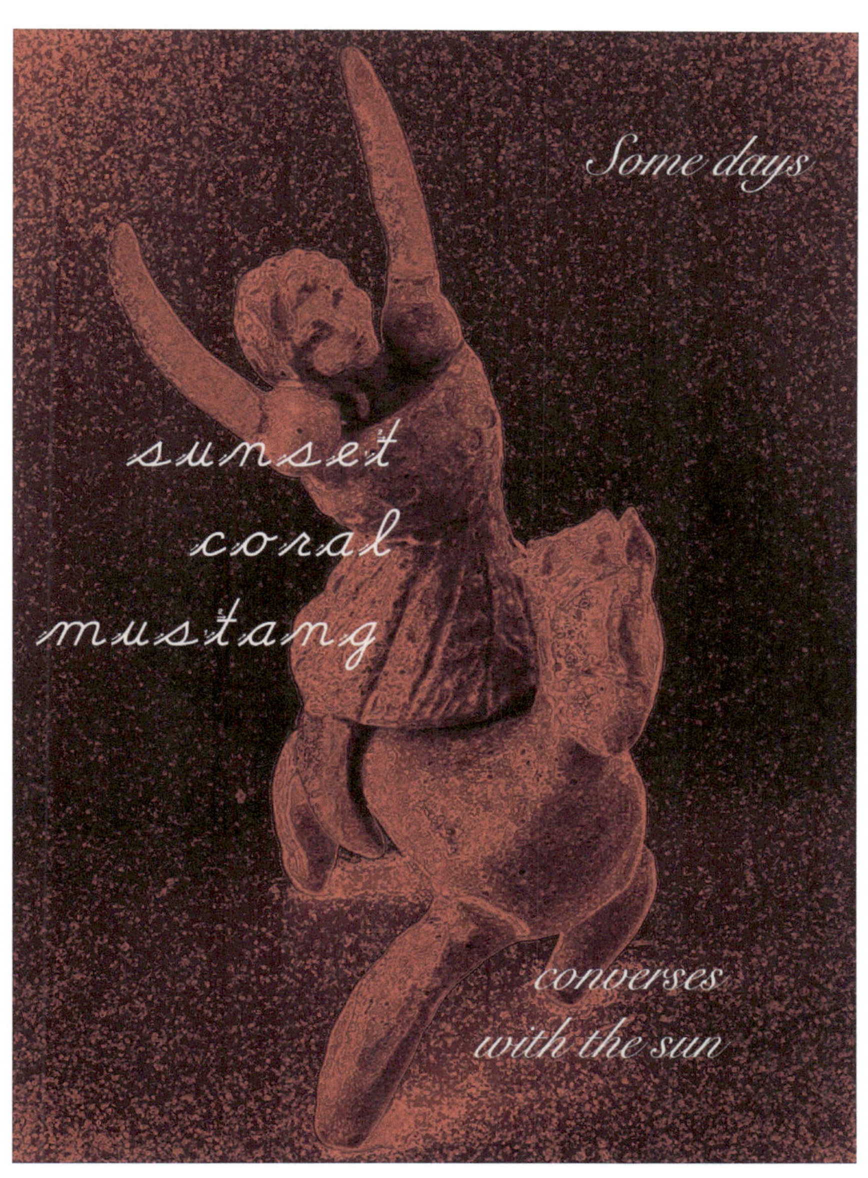
Some days
sunset
coral
mustang
converses
with the sun

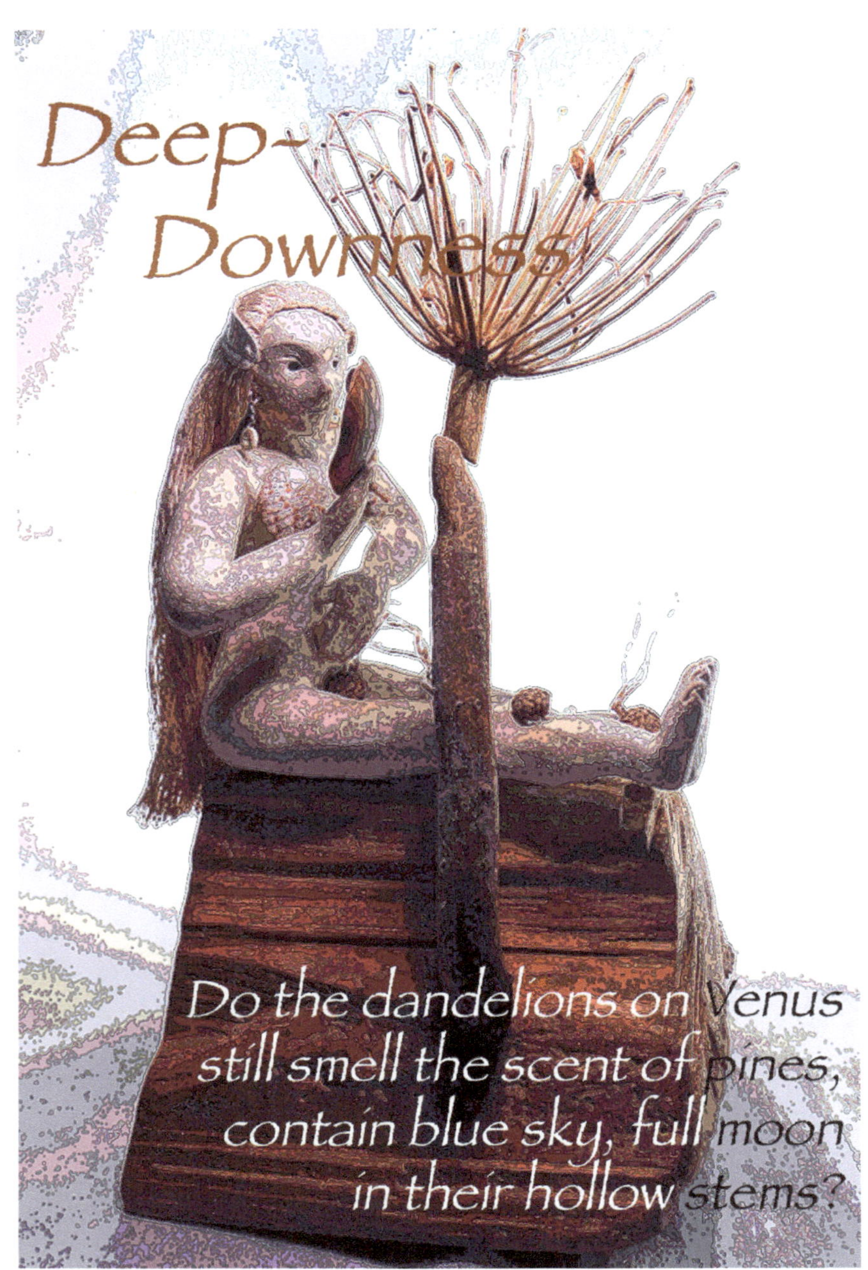
Deep-
Downness
Do the dandelions on Venus
still smell the scent of pines,
contain blue sky, full moon
in their hollow stems?

Deep-Downness

Do the dandelions on Venus
still smell the scent of pines,
contain blue sky, full moon
in their hollow stems?

Rain Stick

hollowed plant
sound

rituals

origin

unclear

thorns push through the stalk
falling objects   inside

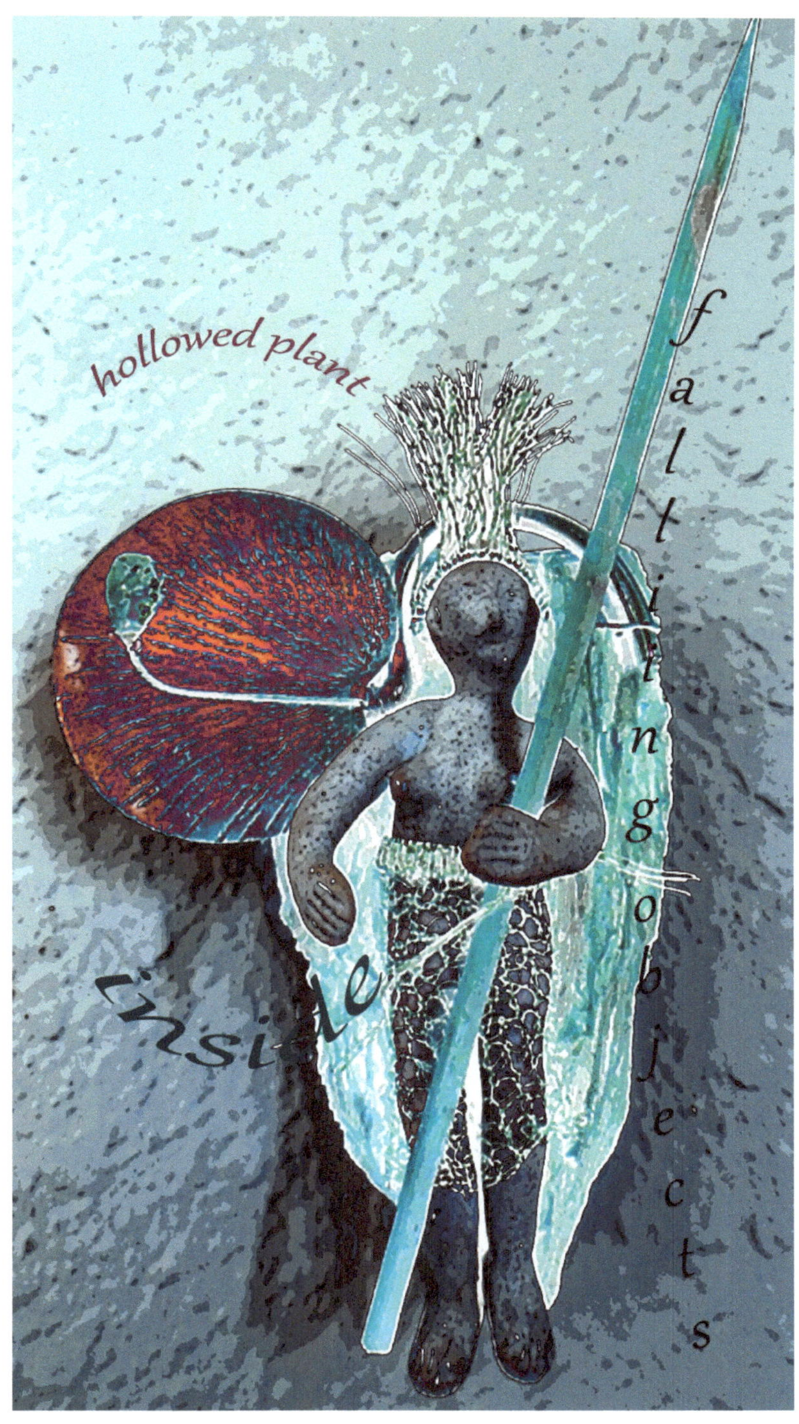
hollowed plant
inside
falling objects

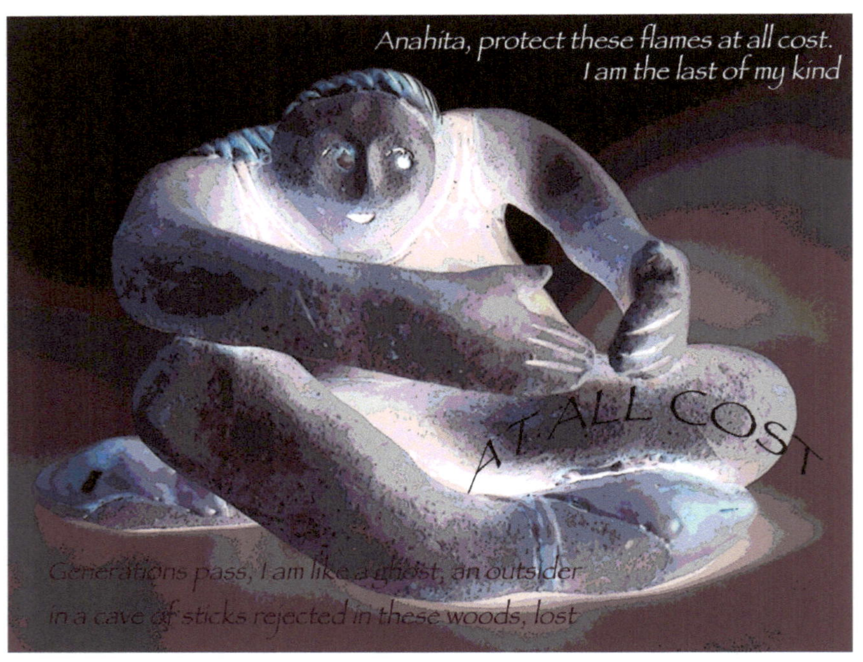
Anahita, protect these flames at all cost.
I am the last of my kind
AT ALL COST
Generations pass, I am like a ghost, an outsider
in a cave of sticks rejected in these woods, lost

At all Cost

Anahita, protect these flames at all cost,
Candleman cries.
I am the last of my kind,
rejected outsider in these woods lost.

Hidden in the frost of decayed logs,I stoop
to protect these flames at all cost.
Generations pass, I am like a ghost, an outsider
in a cave of sticks rejected in these woods, lost.

Return from the Grave

Ancestors
wove birch
branches

slept

persevered
in circadian cycles

rested beneath
quarter
moon

quietly drifted

past thin
papery bark

of hidden
spirit
midwives

after the leaves fell

skeletons
strung

seed necklaces
for newborns

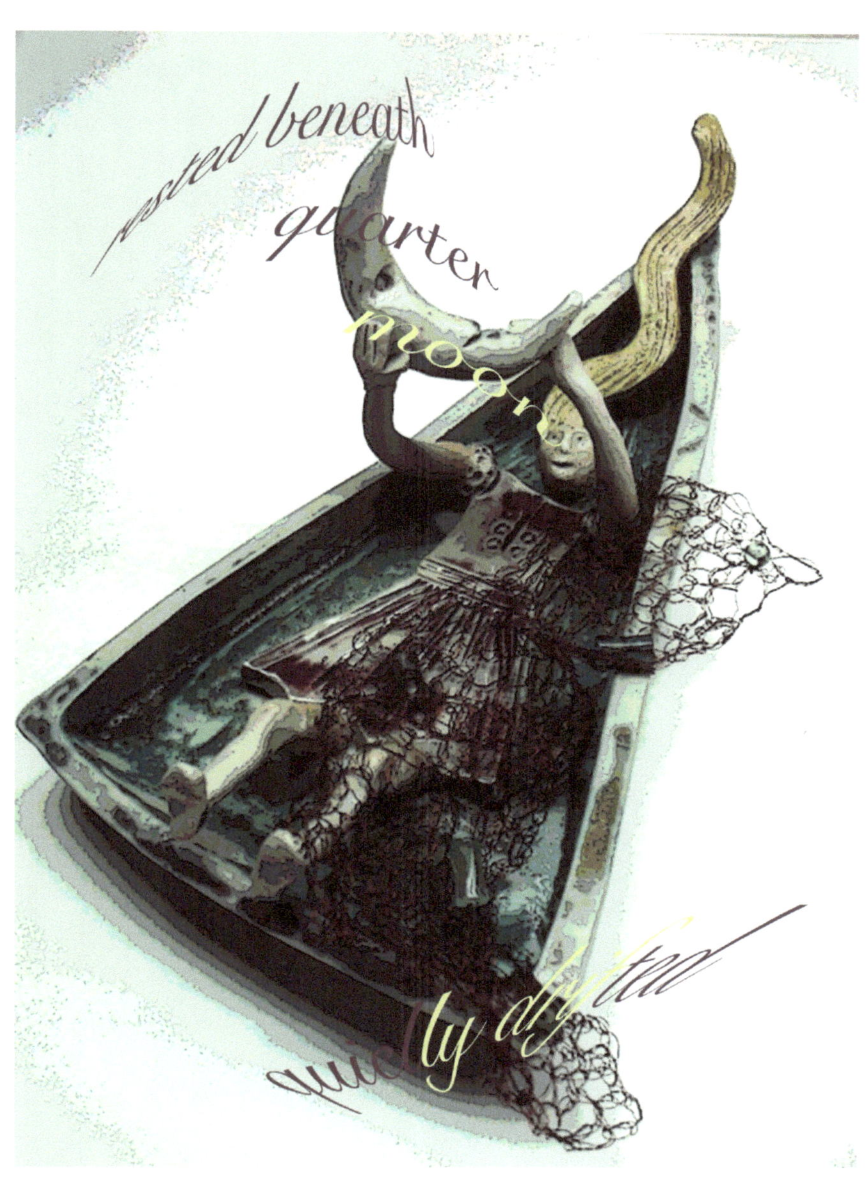
nested beneath
quarter
moon
quietly drifted

Crystalwind Vanishes and Finds a Map

She finds herself in an aspen forest. Blue rain begins to fall as Anahita floats to meet her.

Welcome. I am Anahita. You have arrived into the Map of the Ancestors where bloodlines are drawn as interlaced branches.

The goddess explains, *The map was carved by a wolf-person. You can follow the curves to forecast your life like lines on your palms.*

After all these Years of Waiting

Man of flames slips away while Crystalwind is asleep—
Is she the one? He combs the hillside, stream,
and ventures into the meadow for nature's edible
delights in cosmic colors cultivates food
from starshine for her to eat.

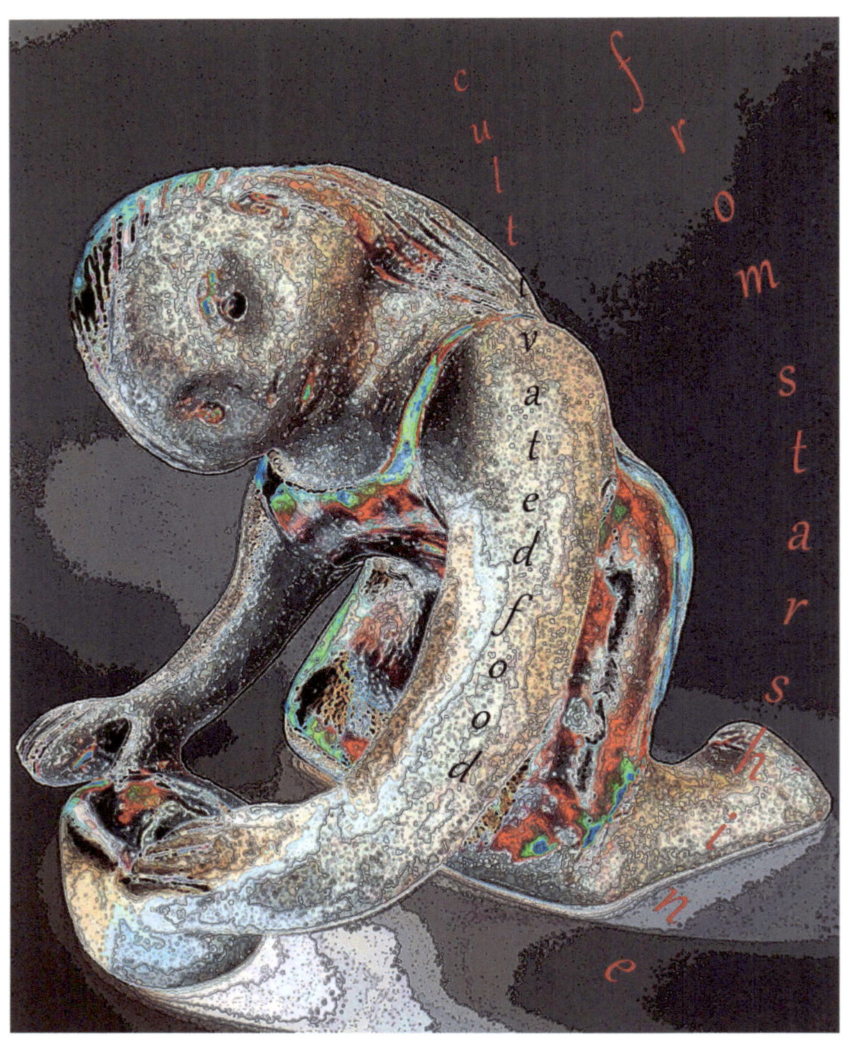
cultivated food
from starshine

Decay

Just when she thought the day had nothing left,
Crystalwind measures spaghetti, hard, sleek.
Her hand wraps a smaller volume without father.

Every Monday is spaghetti day.
No deciding what to cook,
the kids like it.

Suddenly mother finds herself in a pile of branches
and decayed trunks where once a tree flourished.
As fear enters, Mother holds her breath.

She smells wisps of smoke and discovers a soft
glow like a halo. Her eyes adjust. Crystalwind
observes brilliance radiating from several votives.

Gasps as she notices a figure with four arms.
She rubs her eyes to make sure she is looking
at a Candleman.

Thinks of Her Family

Crystalwind closes her eyes, tries to rest, but can't.

As she thrashes about, she pictures Azurite sitting

at the table and chairs that belonged to her parents

under the light fixture made by her father from a wagon

wheel. Azurite helps Moonfox and Dreamstar with homework.

The fire crackles. Azurite pushes aside the gingham curtains

with a swish to gape at the forest and the layered mountains

that form the horizon. Later, it's the stars, a Milky Way display.

And Venus near the moon. Didn't Anahita mention Venus?

Part II

Crystalwind's Family

The Elements

Crystalwind is the fire

Azurite is the water

Moonfox is the earth

Dreamstar is the sky

Merger of Heartbeat & Bark

Memories of her
        meticulous collection of feathers—

pheasant, quail, and blue jay
        taped to cardboard, labeled,
glistening in plastic wrap. Her secret

possession. Later burned like this forest
        home. Decayed wood for a bed and
nestlings will soon cling to the cavity wall.

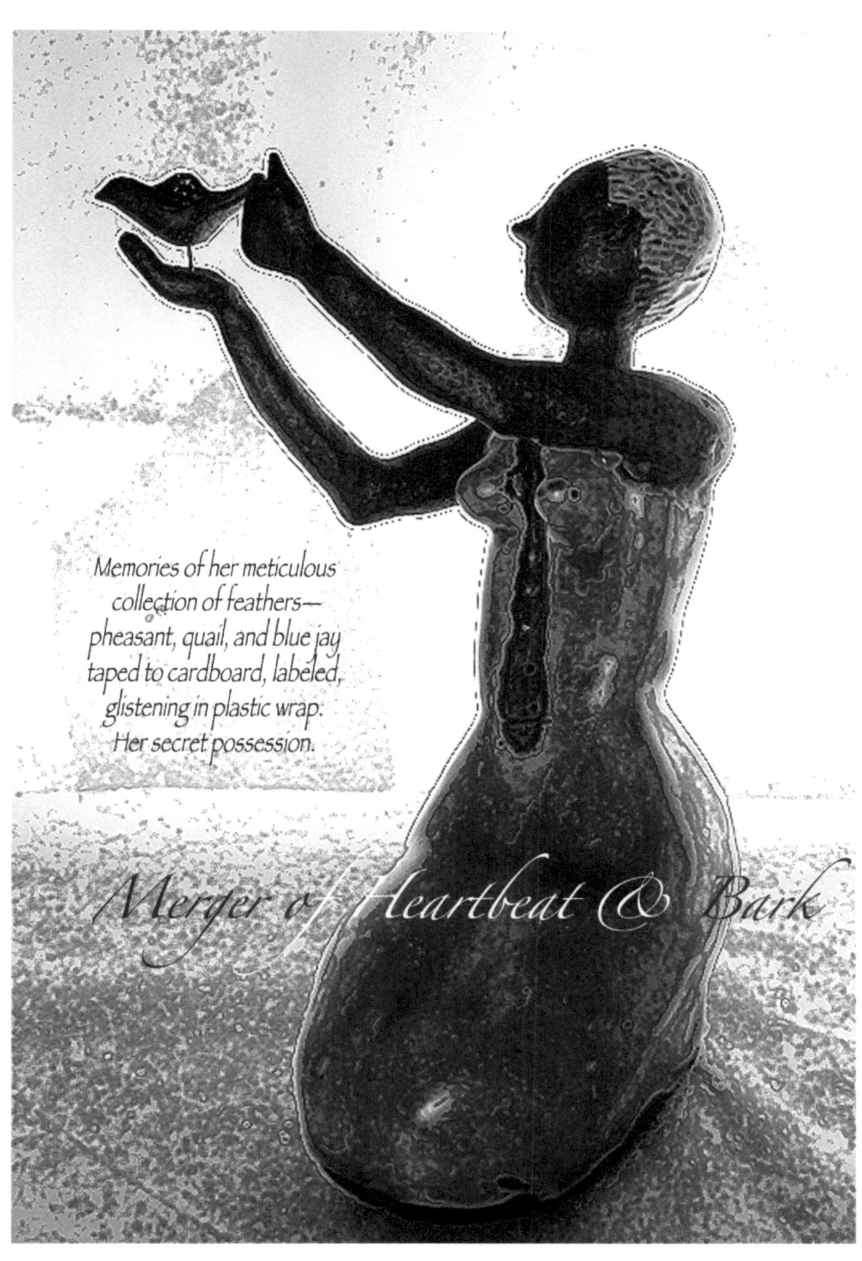
Memories of her meticulous
collection of feathers—
pheasant, quail, and blue jay
taped to cardboard, labeled,
glistening in plastic wrap.
Her secret possession.
Merger of Heartbeat & Bark

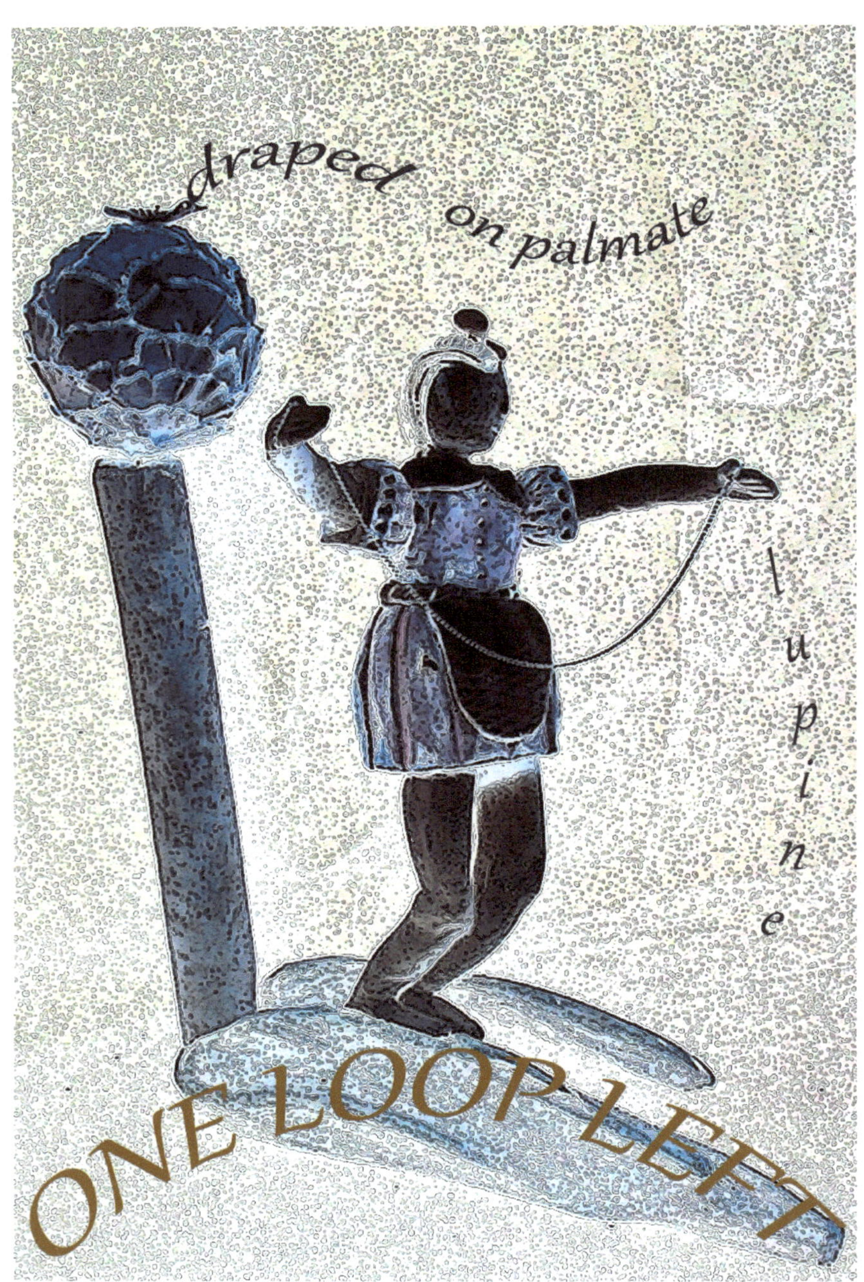
draped on palmate
lupine
ONE LOOP LEFT

The Wolf Flower

Finds her scarab bracelet
draped on palmate lupine
leaves desolate, poisonous,
purple spires. One loop left
of safety chain—
tiger eye, carnelian,
and rose quartz link.

Exposed Roots

rings of time
moss and honey
mushrooms
chisel trunk

I left
your hiking
boots next
to mine
where dirt
still clings

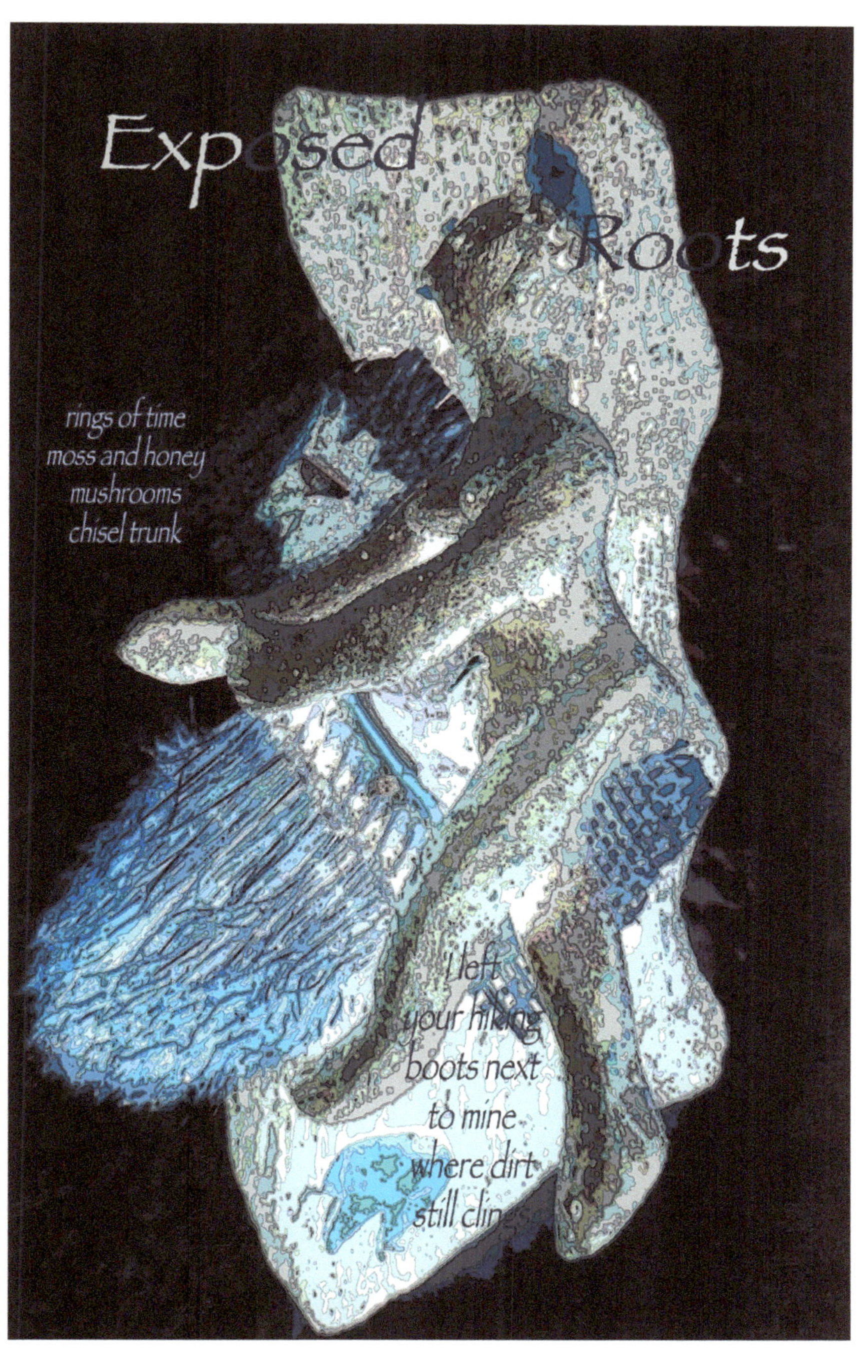
Exposed Roots
rings of time
moss and honey
mushrooms
chisel trunk
i left
your hiking
boots next
to mine
where dirt
still clin

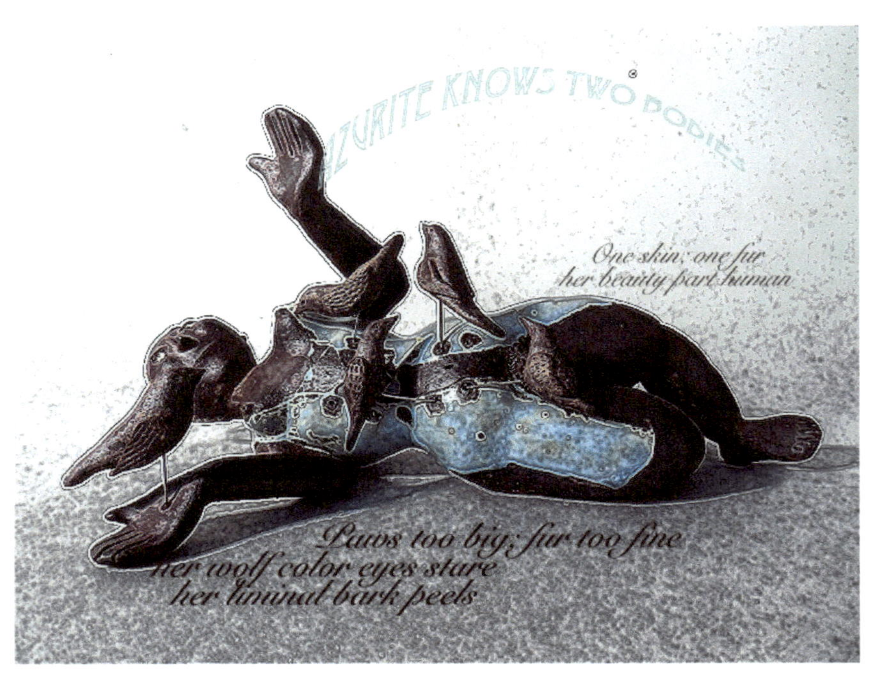
AZURITE KNOWS TWO BODIES
One skin; one fur
her beauty part human
Paws too big; fur too fine
her wolf color eyes stare
her liminal bark peels

Azurite Knows Two Bodies

One skin; one fur
her beauty part human
paws too big; fur too fine
eyes wolf-color stare
her liminal bark peels

No Shortness of Breath

I.
Sierra mule deer looks deep into brother's chestnut eyes. Young, but he sees gentleness and a respect for nature. Deer, gatekeeper to the high places, allows brother and sister to pass.

II.
Moonfox fears owl and feels less afraid with deer. Ready to climb, his pudgy foot slips a couple times on smooth, granite boulders. The wind threatens to take his hat. *Be careful,* says Dreamstar from below. Brother pictures the grace of deer as he scrapes his short fingers. The air is thin, but easy for him to breathe. The incense cedars and white pines arch in biting winds. Brother inhales their spicy smell and takes another step.

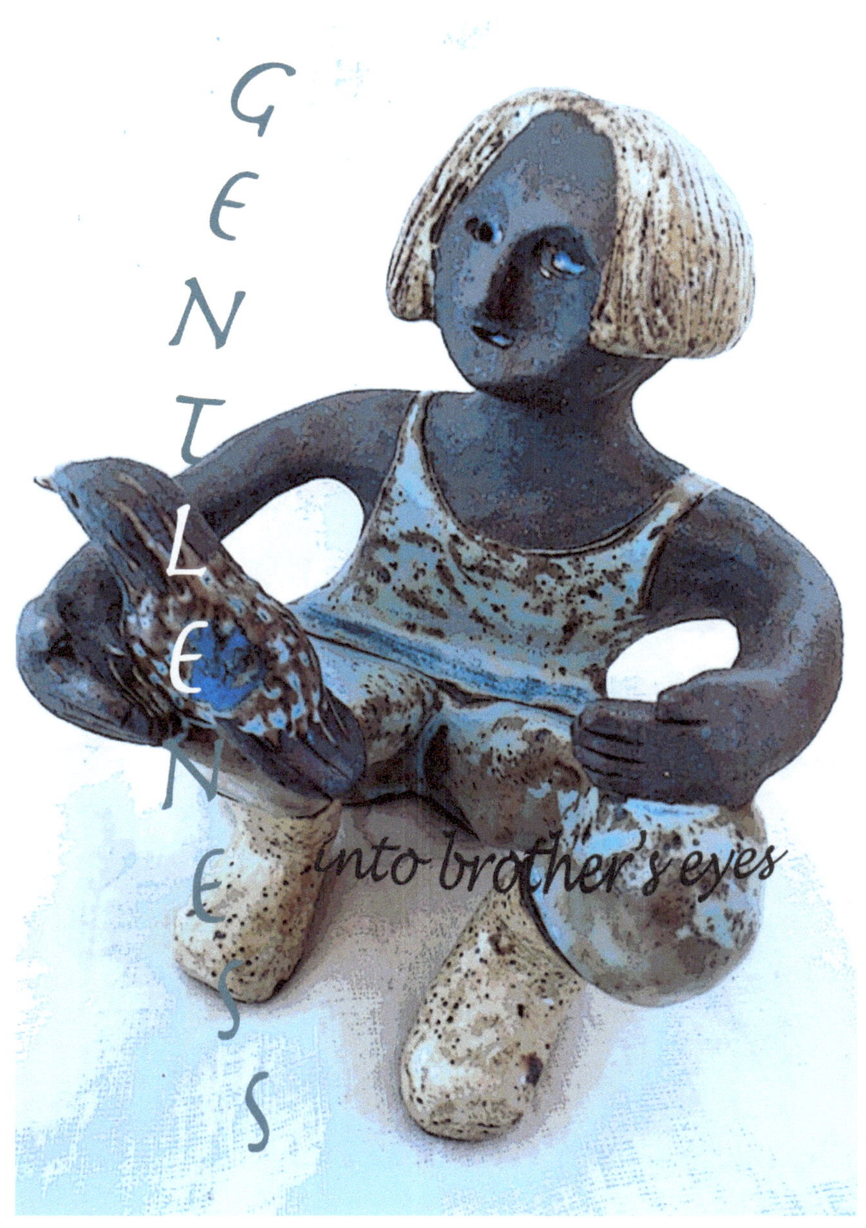
GENTLENESS
into brother's eyes

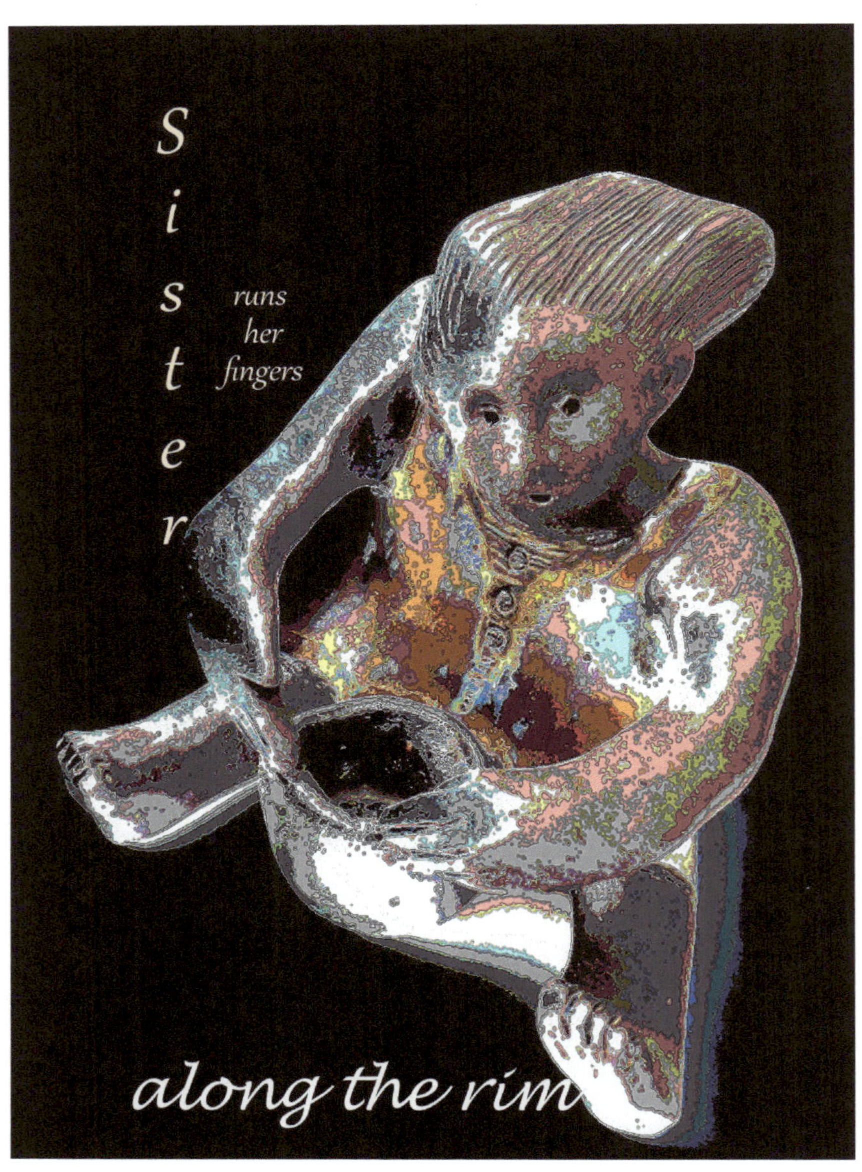
S
i
s
t
e
r
runs
her
fingers
along the rim

Murmurs

Sister runs her fingers along the rim of maize grinding holes
carved long before she was born. Reminds her of how mother

went missing while cooking dinner. Deep breath.
She is brave for brother as she descends towards the roar

of the waterfall. Boulders loom above, beside,
and across the rushing river. Sister is amazed

at a quiet section of the river. Here, dry grasses bend
over gentle mosaic water patterns. She sees the sandy

bottom and tries to hold the tree's shadow. A murmur
gurgles as golden rocks beckon her to climb.

Crystalwind Imagines Anahita

White pine scent
brushes Anahita's arms.
She hikes a foggy hill.
Time suspends.

The goddess rises
into the atmosphere.
Moves the damp clouds
with a swoosh of her left hand.

Her right shifts the prickly sun.
She guides western tanagers
with a glance. Sings as paths
change at her whim.

The End

Acknowledgments

Thank you to the following journals and blogposts in which these poems and art first appeared, some in a slightly different form:

Cholla Needles Arts & Literary Library, "Merger of Heartbeat and Bark" and "Presence / Absence"

Event Horizon Magazine: "Murmurs"

Les Femmes Folles: "At All Cost" and "Today in the Forest"

Yak Press, Poetry Circus Chapbook: "Return from the Grave"

About the Authors

Cindy Rinne creates fiber art and writes in San Bernardino, CA. Cindy is the author of several books: *silence between drumbeats* (Four Feathers Press), *Letters Under Rock* with Bory Thach, (Elyssar Press), and others. Her poetry appeared or is forthcoming: *Anti-Heroin Chic, Verse-Virtual, LitGleam,* and others, plus several anthologies. www.fiberverse.com

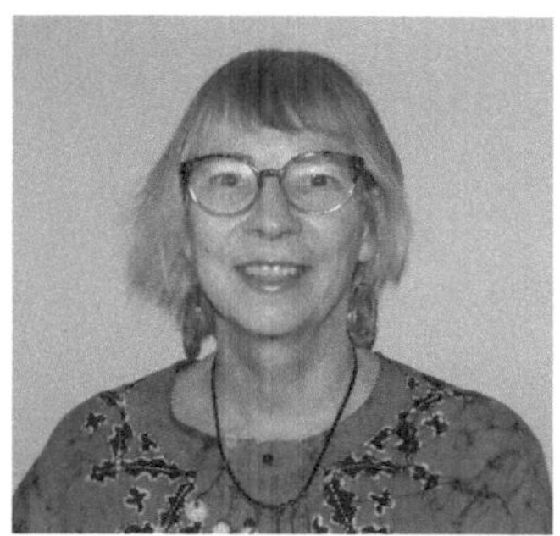

Toti O'Brien's mixed media have been exhibited in group and solo shows, in Europe and the US, since 1995. She has illustrated several children books and two memoirs. Her artwork is on the cover of several books and it was most recently featured in *pethricor, Two Hawks, Arkana* and *Argo*. More about her work can be found at http://totihan.net/index.html

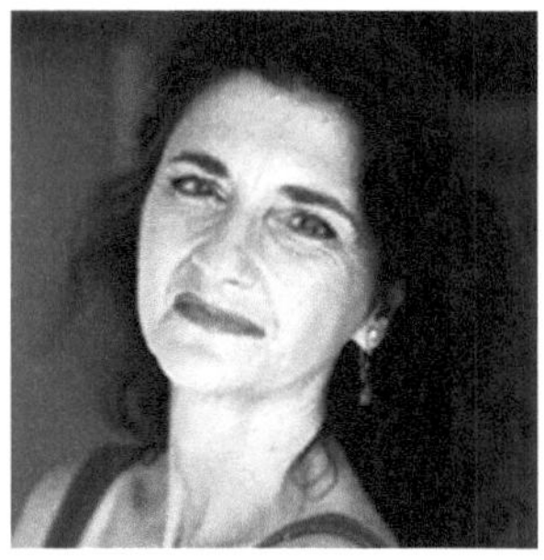

www.ingramcontent.com/pod-product-compliance
Lightning Source LLC
LaVergne TN
LVHW052301100826
845147LV00001B/107